BEHIND THE MASK

REVERSING THE PROCESS OF UNRESOLVED LIFE ISSUES

D0813816

BEHIND THE MASK

REVERSING THE PROCESS OF UNRESOLVED LIFE ISSUES

Bill Thrall, Bruce McNicol and John Lynch
Editor - Mike Hamel

LEADERSHIP
CATALYST

A Leadership Catalyst Resource
www.leadershipcatalyst.org

Leadership Catalyst, Inc.
1600 E. Northern Avenue, Suite 280, Phoenix, AZ 85020
Toll free - 1.888.249.0700   www.leadershipcatalyst.org

Established in 1995, Leadership Catalyst is an international resource for helping people learn how to build and restore trust in their key relationships. Through this resource, many people experience remarkable communities of authenticity, maturity and productivity. These communities are often described by the phrase, "environments of grace."

The vision of Leadership Catalyst is to leave in its wake thousands of high-trust environments of grace. The mission of Leadership Catalyst is to build and restore trust in your key relationships.

Leadership Catalyst Resources are available through our website. Substantial discounts on bulk quantities of LCI resources are available to corporations, professional associations, and other organizations. For details and discount information, contact Leadership Catalyst at 1.888.249.0700, or visit our website at www.leadershipcatalyst.org

ISBN: 0-9770908-1-7

Some of the anecdotal illustrations in this book are true to life and are included with the permission of the persons involved. All other illustrations are composites of real situations, and any resemblance to people living or dead is coincidental.

Printed in Canada

For a free catalog of Leadership Catalyst books and resources, call 1.888.249.0700 or visit LCI online at: www.leadershipcatalyst.org

LEADERSHIP CATALYST

A Leadership Catalyst Resource
www.leadershipcatalyst.org

To all those in the wake of your influence

Thanks to the many who, with courage and a simple trust in Christ, are reversing the process of unresolved life issues.

Bill Thrall, Bruce McNicol and John Lynch

TABLE OF CONTENTS

INTRODUCTION

The material in this little book first appeared in the hardback edition of *TrueFaced, Trust God and Others with Who You Really Are,* published by NavPress. For the second edition, we revised the book into the more streamlined *TrueFaced Experience Edition,* which got to the core themes more quickly.

Our readers soon let us know that some of what we dispensed within the revision was indispensable, especially the material on working through the process set in motion by unresolved sin.

The act of sin—ours or someone else's—creates within us an involuntary response of guilt or hurt, which leads to the inevitable effects of pain, turmoil, and mask wearing. Understanding this three-phase process and learning how to escape from it, is what *Behind the Mask* is all about.

The truths in *Behind the Mask* will have far greater impact if applied in the context of pursuing your God-ordained destiny as outlined in the *TrueFaced Experience Edition* book, the *TrueFaced Experience Guide* and the *TrueFaced Experience* DVD. See the back of the book for ordering details.

CHAPTER ONE
WHY THE MASK?

There is a face that we hide
Till the nighttime appears,
And what's hiding inside,
Behind all of our fears,
Is our true self
Locked inside the façade!

—Jekyll and Hyde

MOST OF US WILL ADMIT TO WEARING MASKS
BUT WE HAVE NO IDEA HOW TO TAKE THEM OFF.
WE ARE IN THE DARK ABOUT HOW WE GOT LIKE
THIS. WE BLAME OUR ACTIONS ON CIRCUM-
STANCES OR THE PRESSURE WE'RE UNDER.

Over time, most of us notice that our struggles with sin are not going away. In fact, we have to paste more and more layers on the mask we hide behind just to hold it together. Our real thoughts, emotions and behaviors—which are threatening and inappropriate—scare us. So we say things we don't believe and pretend to like things we dislike. Some of us have become human time bombs—resentful, guarded and ready to blow. We need a lot of down time to be alone, free from the pressure of pretending.

Those around us know something's wrong. Family or friends worry that it might have something to do with the masks they're wearing. Others have stopped trying to work through any problems or concerns they have with us; they have learned not to bring up things that push our hot buttons. "Don't try to talk to him about . . ." "Don't ever bring up . . ." Eventually they stop risking intimacy with us. They tiptoe around us. "He's too thorny, too erratic." "She's too defensive, too unpredictable."

Most of us will admit to wearing masks but we have no idea how to take them off. We are in the dark about how we got like this. We blame our actions on circumstances or the pressure we're under.

What we need to see is what causes the responses that trip us up. We need to come to the realization that our controlling behavior isn't just a response to something happening right now. It was triggered by multiple unresolved sin issues from

> **IF WE HAVE SINNED, OUR INVOLUNTARY RESPONSE IS CALLED GUILT. IF OTHERS HAVE SINNED AGAINST US, OUR INVOLUNTARY RESPONSE IS CALLED HURT.**

the past. When we begin to understand the progression of unresolved sin and what it does, we might no longer react to life like lemmings heading for a cliff.

This chapter is meant to be used as a diagnostic tool to reveal where the problem is and what may have caused it.

WHAT UNRESOLVED SIN DOES TO THE HEART

No car ever started moving simply because someone turned a key. The key triggered something, which caused something else to fire, which forced some other something to rotate, eventually starting the engine.

In a similar way, an unresolved act of sin can trigger a predictable and uncompromising three-phase process:

> Act of Sin
>
> Involuntary Response
>
> Inevitable Effect

Sin sets the ball in motion. Someone sins against us or we sin against someone else, and that act of sin evokes within us an involuntary response. We don't have to work at producing these responses. They are automatic. If we have sinned, our involuntary response is called guilt. If others have sinned against us, our involuntary response is called hurt.

God designed these responses to get our attention.

BOTH THE ONE WHO SINS AND THE ONE SINNED
AGAINST HAVE AN INVOLUNTARY HEART
RESPONSE TO AN ACT OF SIN. IN THE ONE WHO
SINS, THE EFFECT IS GUILT. IN THE ONE WHO IS
SINNED AGAINST, THE EFFECT IS HURT.

Something has been broken and needs healing. However, many
of us cover up our guilt or hurt because we don't know
what to do with our responses. If we hide or try to override
our guilt or hurt—if we do not move toward resolution—life
gets very bad in a hurry. Our involuntary responses will
progress to inevitable effects, unleashing a new depth of pain,
inner turmoil, and mask-wearing.

Most of us never tie together the act of sin, the involuntary
responses, and the inevitable effects. We are not aware of the
chain reaction. We only know we are carrying feelings,
thoughts, and behaviors we can't figure out and feel a need
to mask. But our futile disguise simply tells others we have
problems. They have no more idea than we do about why
we're acting so oddly. They just pity us. Or talk about us. Or
they find socially acceptable ways to keep their distance. We're
like a tourist trying to impress his waiter by bluffing fluency in
another language, unaware that instead of medallions of lamb
he just ordered a dish of metal fasteners. He unwittingly
becomes the subject of much ridicule and mockery back in the
kitchen.

Wouldn't it be great to discover how to stop this three-phase
chain reaction? Wouldn't it be awesome to discover how our
cracking mask could actually be removed to expose the wonderful face God has always wanted to reveal? Wouldn't it be
incredibly fantastic to have that kind of hope?

Hope begins by understanding this critical point: Both the
one who sins and the one sinned against have an involuntary
heart response to an act of sin. In the one who sins, the effect is
guilt. In the one who is sinned against, the effect is hurt.

IN THE ONE WHO SINS: **GUILT**

Guilt is a good thing. God has graciously etched a bench-
mark in our hearts. A standard. God calls it a conscience. It
roars to life in order to make us aware of sin we have committed.
When we do something wrong, we feel guilt, at least initially.
Guilt yells, "Hey pal, pay attention to this. If you think
guilt feels lousy, just try to ignore it and see what follows!" If
we don't recognize the purpose of the guilt—to prompt us to
resolve our sin—we may just forget to deal with our sin.
Eventually the incident will fade from our memory and our
guilt loses its sharp edge. We would rather ignore our sin than
acknowledge that we did something wrong, so we stuff the
guilt we feel.
But here's what happens. In stuffing our guilt, we avoid
admitting that what we did deeply harmed and impacted
another. Our sin hurt someone. The decision to ignore our sin
creates unresolved sin, which is like an undiagnosed disease that
quietly spreads poison throughout our bloodstream. We may
recognize we don't have the energy we used to have, but we
blame this on something or someone else and fail to recognize
that an invisible, inner enemy drains our energy and joy. This
destructive sequence occurs because, even though we tried to
bury it, our unresolved sin remains very much alive.

WHY THE MASK?

C   H   A   P   T   E   R   O   N   E

LEFT UNRESOLVED, ONE ACT OF SIN LAYS THE
GROUNDWORK FOR SERIOUS RELATIONAL
BREAKDOWNS.

When an act of known sin remains unresolved, it causes a
nagging sense in the heart that doesn't go away. To resolve this
sin, we need to access God's resources for dealing with what we
know we have done and with what our actions have done to
others. Of course, resolving a sin doesn't mean we'll never
struggle with it again. It only means we've stopped its present
path of destruction and are living in health. It means we're
addressing a particular known act of sin, openly and specifical-
ly, in a safe environment.

Many of us avoid dealing with how our sin affects others
because we can't face the reality of what it says about us. "I
can't be known as a person who does that kind of thing." Or
perhaps we are not convinced God can help or heal us. Like
plaque, unresolved sin builds up. Eventually we have so much
junk in our lives that we're convinced God can barely tolerate
us. Left unresolved, one act of sin lays the groundwork for
serious relational breakdowns.

IN THE ONE SINNED AGAINST: **HURT**

Meanwhile, the one who sustains the impact of sin experiences hurt or violation. Nothing in us enables us to absorb the
sin done against us and the resulting hurt. Nothing.

This makes most of us want to scream, "But that isn't fair. I
was not the one who sinned." And we're right. It is not fair. Sin
is not fair. But, when we are sinned against and we don't know

how to resolve that sin, it will always ignite the nature of the sin already in us. We, the hurt ones, now give ourselves permission to act out sinfully. Twisted, isn't it?

This hurt is also a very good thing. God made us to feel hurt so that we would go to him for healing. But that's a pretty fragile thing to do—to admit that we feel hurt. It feels like we are giving in to our offender—letting him or her off the hook.

So instead of going to God, we tell ourselves, "I'll be fine. I just need to move on. I'm fine . . . really." So, we walk on, unconsciously adding to the unresolved hurt of dozens of other sins committed against us. Meanwhile, we don't know why we feel so angry, depressed, and bitter.

Want some good news? We can stop the damage of sin done against us by applying God's resources and power to resolve that sin. Remember, this can be a place of hope. But if we don't access God's resources, the devastating pattern continues.

HOW GUILT AND HURT MUTATE

When we trust our own ideas about how to handle our guilt or hurt, we allow something much worse to be released in us. Suddenly, our guilt or hurt morphs into half a dozen or more ugly inevitable effects. Guilt and hurt turn into shame, blame, fear, denial, and anger.

If we don't resolve the sin that caused the guilt or hurt, it will inflame sin within us—even if the sin was not initially ours. Guilt or hurt, those wonderful God-given gifts, have mutated into inevitable effects that are nothing but harmful. When too much pressure on a dam produces a crack, it must be

WE VIEW LIFE THROUGH A SELF-PROTECTIVE
GRID THAT PRODUCES ANY NUMBER OF
INEVITABLE EFFECTS, INCLUDING SHAME, BLAME,
FEAR, DENIAL, AND ANGER. NONE OF THESE
"JUST HAPPEN" TO APPEAR IN OUR HEARTS. WE
PLANTED THE SEEDS OURSELVES AND WATERED
THEM.

sealed or the water behind the dam inevitably floods the village
below. Similarly, our choice to go our own way at the involuntary response phase propels us into the unstoppable—the
inevitable effects.

This process plays out in every person, even those who don't
claim to follow Christ. The only real difference between this
group and Christ followers is the hope of a solution. But if
Christians refuse that hope, we lay ourselves open to an endless
variety of bogus remedies: conscience numbing medication,
pop psychology, spiritual fads, and other nicely packaged
placebos. Whenever we sin and don't resolve it, either because
we don't know how or choose not to, we release an inevitable
force that will drain confidence in who we really are.

Now we need a primo mask, maybe several. We hastily
choose from dozens of options: "I'm better than most," "I'm
very together," "I don't really care," "I am self-sufficient,"
"I have the answers." But still our heart whispers: "You're an
impostor, a loser. You always have been, always will be.
You're a joke, a hypocrite. You have no self-respect. You spent it
long ago."

A SAMPLING OF INEVITABLE EFFECTS

So now, we enter a new land of coping, covering, plotting, and reacting. We view life through a self-protective grid that produces any number of inevitable effects, including shame, blame, fear, denial, and anger. None of these "just happen" to appear in our hearts. We planted the seeds ourselves and watered them. They are poisonous weeds that can only be pulled by God. Until we let him, they will shape how we see our lives.

Let's take a closer look at some of the most common and significant inevitable effects. Not every unresolved sin produces every effect. And we may experience two or more of these effects simultaneously from the same unresolved sin.

SHAME

Unresolved guilt and hurt produce shame. When Adam and Eve violated God's command and then refused to take responsibility for their sin, they experienced the shame of their own nakedness. This shame, this self-perception of embarrassment and being "dirty," prompted them to fashion a mask from fig leaves to hide what was true about them.

Guilt makes us aware of sin and evokes in us a feeling of shame when we don't resolve that sin. And, like Adam, we instinctively fashion masks to cover our shame. Only when we accept God's covering can we break this pattern.

Hurt makes us aware that we have been sinned against. Not

GUILT MAKES US AWARE OF SIN AND EVOKES IN
US A FEELING OF SHAME WHEN WE DON'T
RESOLVE THAT SIN.

all violations result in hurt, but when someone sins against us
and we feel hurt, and we do not resolve that sin, we will feel
demeaned and humiliated. It doesn't matter that we did not
commit the initial sin. Whenever we fail to access God's healing
resources and power to resolve a sin—even sin committed
against us—unresolved sin will inflame shame in us.

BLAME

Back to the garden. The Lord confronts Adam and Eve with
their actions and they both humbly take the hit for the other.
Yeah, right! When God confronts Adam, Adam blames Eve.
"The woman . . . she gave me from the tree, and I ate." But
he's not done; he goes right to the top—he blames God! "The
woman you put here with me . . ." Eve, not to be outdone,
blames the serpent. It's a veritable blame fest. It's surprising
the serpent doesn't blame the tree!

When we sin, we often try to absolve ourselves of the guilt
by shifting the blame to another. We can blame others because
we feel shame or we can feel shame because of blame. When
we are sinned against, we frequently do something similar.
We begin to view ourselves as victims and develop a victim's
mindset, blaming who we are on what others have done to us.
We're convinced we have no choice in whom we are and that
we are no longer responsible for our inappropriate reactions.
We are the victim of all we survey.

FEAR

So God comes in the cool of the day to be with Adam and
Eve, but the disobedient duo has gone into hiding. He calls,
and Adam responds, "I heard the sound of you in the garden,
and I was afraid because I was naked; so I hid myself." How
ironic. Because of his sin, Adam feared the one who'd created
him, the one who loved him and sought him out.

Fear—an inevitable effect of unresolved sin—creates a barrier
in relationships. When we sin against others, it prompts us to
hide from them. We may not hide from them physically, but
we hide socially and emotionally. This cheapens our relationships because we lose the transparency that deepens the bonds
of love. We hide behind a mask that says, "Nothing I do seems
to make a difference."

We fear others. We worry that they will discover our hidden
life. We fear they will confront us with our unresolved sin.
We dread their contempt. We are afraid they will reject us or
speak to others about us. Ironically, we fear the very ones God
designed to love us. That is true irony—we hide from what
will heal us.

Those hurt by acts of sin also experience this inevitable
effect and, out of fear, try to hide from others. Their hurt has
convinced them that others cannot and should not be trusted.
It causes them to believe there must be something about them
that gives an offender the right to hurt them. They keep everyone out—even those who could love them and help them heal.

THOSE HURT BY ACTS OF SIN ALSO EXPERIENCE
THIS INEVITABLE EFFECT AND, OUT OF FEAR,
TRY TO HIDE FROM OTHERS. THEIR HURT HAS
CONVINCED THEM THAT OTHERS CANNOT AND
SHOULD NOT BE TRUSTED.

DENIAL

Unresolved guilt or hurt can also make us vulnerable to patterns of denial. We find no joy in admitting we are sinners—that is way too risky. Nor do we find joy in admitting we are hurting—that also feels too risky. We already feel at the edge of other people's acceptance. We can't let another thing be added to the list, or they may reassess our worthiness for their friendship.

Denial keeps us from facing the truth about ourselves. If we are the offender, it allows us to deny that we've done anything wrong. If we are the offended, it allows us to deny that the sin done to us has affected us. If we have unresolved guilt, our denial can range from lying about our actions to refusing to acknowledge the consequences of our sin on the other person. "Come on, you're making a big deal out of nothing. I said I was sorry!" If we have unresolved hurt, we will deny we've been hurt. Such an admission would make us too fragile, too vulnerable. So, we try to deny any pain, hurt, or violation.

People who live in denial refuse to give permission to others to speak about the things everyone else can see. Those in denial insist that friends agree with their assessments and rewriting of history. Inside their fortress, those in denial are becoming self-vindicating judges. They are alone and secretly terrified, because they know the truth of what they deny.

"ANGER AND CONTEMPT ARE THE TWIN
SCOURGES OF THE EARTH."

ANGER

Anger brings a heroic sense of purpose to our guilt or our hurt. It gives us energy, explosive and unpredictable energy. Anger that comes from guilt says, "I'm tired of taking the fall all the time because somebody reacted badly to something I did or said." And now, we are on our way to producing more acts of sin, leading to more guilt, breeding even more anger.

Our society is full of this kind of accumulating rage. Dallas Willard writes, "Anger and contempt are the twin scourges of the earth." Anger that comes from hurt says, "I am experiencing a life I do not deserve. I was unfairly hurt. I demand a hearing. I want to use every means I have to make somebody pay. If no one else is going to admit that I have been treated unfairly, including God, then I will bring others to justice."

Many people say, "I just don't know why I get so angry." Most often, they don't know because they have never traced their anger back to its root—unresolved sin, from either hurt or guilt. They also don't know because anger is blind. It cannot see truth very well—the truth of anger's resolution. Anger has a limited and distorted perspective. It thinks, because I'm hurt, I must be right. Anger holds court without evidence or witnesses and carries only the perspective of the presumed innocent party. Even if we are partially responsible for the wrong we've experienced, our anger hides this fact.

SHARON'S STORY

To help us explain just how destructive this three-phase process can be, we've asked a good friend to tell her story.

Sharon grew up in a family well respected for its great teachers, worship leaders, and community pillars. As a young girl, she sang beautifully and played a number of instruments proficiently. Poised, attractive, intelligent, and charming, Sharon had enormous potential and passion. But as she became a young adult, every now and then she would unexpectedly erupt in rage over something insignificant.

As Sharon became an adult, she gained responsibilities that matched her growing proficiency. But she didn't smile as much or as easily. She found herself lashing out at her new husband and then feeling terrible. Outsiders saw Sharon as a role model, but to those close to her, she was an enigma. When she entered her thirties, much of Sharon's kindness was replaced with a growing air of superiority. She grew incredibly driven, and spent more time alone.

What could cause these increasing displays of pain in a seemingly together person? Based on the phases of unresolved sin, what would we expect to find beneath the surface? What acts of sin? What involuntary responses might create a mix of such competency wrapped in dysfunction? Let Sharon tell you:

I grew up attending church each time the doors were open, and I trusted Jesus as my savior as a very young girl. But what I heard in church and what I experienced at home were two very different things. My "Christian" parents sinned violently against me. My father and many other men used me sexually, and my mother knew of it. Whenever I resisted, my parents

BECAUSE I DID NOT KNOW HOW TO RESOLVE MY
HURT, A TORRENT OF INEVITABLE EFFECTS WAS
UNLEASHED IN MY LIFE.

would twist Scripture by saying that children are to obey their parents "in all things."

My parents did further harm by repeatedly telling me I was born with the "wrong personality" and that no man would ever want to marry me because I was too strong. I knew that God had created me to be a leader, but my parents did their best to crush those qualities in my personality.

As a child I wasn't able to bring to God the acts of sin done against me. I couldn't even understand what was happening to me and didn't know what to do with the involuntary responses of hurt and guilt. Because I did not know how to resolve my hurt, a torrent of inevitable effects was unleashed in my life.

The sexual abuse left me with physical scars. Because I was just a child, I felt I must have done something to deserve the abuse, and this false guilt made me feel shame. I felt that I didn't deserve to be looked upon with anything but contempt.

My shame caused me to grow up believing I was unlovable. Why else would someone violate a little girl so often? I was only worthy to be used and hated.

I was desperately trying to be the right kind of woman, but I had no idea how to act because I didn't even understand who I was. But the deepest wound was my heart's lack of hope that anyone could ever love me. I had no idea what to do with the constant hurt and pain.

Of course, I had to hide the truth of my life. Hiding became the goal of my existence. I did everything I could to control my circumstances. I learned to change my behavior to fit the spiritual culture of wherever I was. I became very judgmental of others so that I could feel better about myself. If I felt anger, I could always blame someone or something for it. I was very good at blaming.

My self-protective behaviors gave me an illusion of safety, but they also kept me from getting my real needs met. I had allowed the sin done to me to inflame my own sin—and I didn't know what to do about it. I didn't trust anyone. I felt alone, unsafe, and unlovable, long after I was far from my parents' home.

Out of God's abundant grace, I got married and had two children. But I could not wear my mask all the time. I couldn't keep up the façade of the godly woman. I unleashed my anger at home. I felt hypocritical, because I wasn't the same person at home that I projected at church.

Finally I decided I no longer wanted to keep pretending to be someone I wasn't. I was finally around people who wanted me to be the person I was created to be, but I had absolutely no idea how to do it! The hurt, buried under my anger, was trying to surface and I didn't know how to go to God with it. I was bitter at my parents and my siblings. I was resentful of my husband for not meeting my needs. I was everything I didn't want to be, and it caused me to feel even more unlovable. And I couldn't stop it.

Things have changed dramatically for Sharon. Her full story can be found in the book *TrueFaced Experience Edition*, along with the powerful truths that have transformed her life.

WHAT ABOUT YOU?

It's time to put this little book down and ask:

) Have I gone down a road leading to shame, blame, fear, denial, and anger?

) Has someone close to me walked down that road without the foggiest idea how to come back home?

Don't rush over these questions. Don't be afraid to admit if you have been so needy. Look fully into the mirror and don't walk away. If you stop long enough to see yourself, the rest of this book will be cool water in a dry and weary land. God says to you, "Hello, my dear child. I've missed you. Welcome home."

DID YOU DISCOVER?

) An unresolved sin is a known sin that creates a nagging sense in the heart that doesn't go away.

) An unresolved act of sin can trigger a predictable and uncompromising three-phase process: Act of Sin, Involuntary Response, Inevitable Effect.

) Hope begins by understanding this critical point: Both the one who sins and the one sinned against have an involuntary response of the heart to an act of sin.

) In the one who sins, the effect is guilt.

) In the one who is sinned against, the effect is hurt.

▶ The decision to ignore our sin creates unresolved sin, which is like an undiagnosed disease that quietly spreads poison throughout our bloodstream.

▶ We can stop the damage of an act of sin done against us at any time by applying God's resources and power to resolve that sin.

▶ Our choice to go our own way at the involuntary response phase propels us into the uncontrollable and unstoppable—the inevitable effects. A sampling of five:

▶ Shame can result from either unresolved guilt or unresolved hurt.

▶ Blame is used to try to absolve ourselves of the guilt caused by our sin.

▶ Fear creates barriers in relationships.

▶ Denial keeps us from facing the truth about ourselves.

▶ Anger has a limited and distorted perspective. It thinks, "Because I'm hurt, I must be right."

CHAPTER TWO
CUSTOM-MADE MASKS

Oh, what a tangled web we weave,
when first we practice to deceive.

—Sir Walter Scott

Each of us brings into every encounter our own personal history, temperament, personality, wounding, influences and previously unresolved sin. And when we don't access God's remedy to deal with sin, those ugly, destructive involuntary effects join forces inside us like oily characters from a gangster movie:

(Read the following dialogue with a cheesy accent.)

"Hey, Shame, look who the cat just drug in!" "Well, I'll be, Guilt. It's Denial and his weasly little buddies, Fear and Anger! Hey, how youse guys doin'? I ain't seen youse around these parts since this sap's little tax indiscretion in '98. Whaddaya say we work together again? Workin' alone ain't much fun. I mean, what good is Denial unless Shame's hangin' around to sweeten the pot? Anger don't get much mileage without Guilt fuelin' the fire. Whaddaya say, guys? We could make this guy a wreck. Imagine Guilt, Denial, Fear, Anger, and Shame workin' against him. He'll be so wigged out, his hair could catch fire and he'd pretend everything's just fine. Let's get to work, boys."

It's hard to predict which inevitable effects will follow from which involuntary responses. This is not an exact science. Let's take a look at six of the dozens of damaging behaviors we engage in when the inevitable effects join forces inside us:

❯ We become highly sensitized to our sin and judge the sin of others.

❯ We lose our objectivity in a crisis and we become the issue.

❯ We hide our sinful behavior and become vulnerable to more sin.

❯ We are unable to be loved or to love.

❯ We become susceptible to wrong life choices.

❯ We attempt to control others.

THE ONE WITH THE KEEN SENSITIVITY TO SIN IS OFTEN THE ONE WITHOUT THE ABILITY TO DEAL WITH THAT SIN!

WE BECOME HIGHLY SENSITIZED TO OUR SIN AND JUDGE THE SIN OF OTHERS

When we are unable or unwilling to resolve the sin within ourselves, we become deeply sensitized toward our sin and the sins of others. We become self-appointed judges of what's wrong with others. Our shame causes us to find blame in them. Like Inspector Javert, the law-obsessed police officer in *Les Misérables*, we become fixated on making sure others pay for what they have done.

If our newfound sensitivity to sin gave us greater ability to resolve the sin in our lives, that would be one thing, but this is not what happens. The one with the keen sensitivity to sin is often the one without the ability to deal with that sin! When this inevitable effect plays itself out in our lives, our sensitivity to our sin and the sins of others causes us to create legalistic and controlling environments. When this is true in families, this damaging pattern can be passed on from generation to generation.

Years of directing Christian summer high-school camps gave Bruce and Bill an incredible desire to discover how to break the patterns of generational dysfunction they saw in the lives of kids. They discovered that the teenagers with the greatest scars were those who came from Christian homes with intense religious control. These kids lived without expressed love and it scarred their souls. They were unable to trust others. They had no solution for the hopelessness in

THOSE WITH SENSITIVITY TO SIN WITHOUT
THE POWER OF GRACE TO DEAL WITH IT—RUIN
THE SPIRIT AND DEEPLY VIOLATE THE SOUL OF
THOSE THEY CLAIM TO LOVE AND ARE
RESPONSIBLE TO LOVE.

their hearts. The very God who alone had answers was, in their minds, no answer at all.

Sara was one of those campers. She came from a Christian home with a strict, legalistic father and a passive, compliant mother. Sixteen, bright, and attractive, Sara knew all the right answers, yet she grew up believing she was never good enough. She saw herself as unlovable.

At camp Sara was quiet and brooding, unwilling to have anything to do with the Bible because her dad had used it to justify his condemnation of her. He displayed no trust in her, offered no praise. Sadly, Sara learned her father's lessons well. Today she turns to drugs and sex to numb the pain in her soul.

What a sick transfer! Those judged actually begin to believe that they deserve the guilt they feel or the shame they bear. People like Sara's father—those with sensitivity to sin without the power of grace to deal with it—ruin the spirit and deeply violate the soul of those they claim to love and are responsible to love.

Those we influence will be affected by what is true in us, no matter how well we think we are hiding. They will bear the brunt of our sensitivity to our sin, because they will bear our judgment. Then, shame, blame, fear, and anger combine in them to create another generation of distorted sensitivity to the sin in others.

You mean that's why my children and those I influence learn my behaviors and copy my dysfunctions? Children become

WHEN WE HAVE UNRESOLVED SIN ISSUES,
THE PRESSURE OF A CRISIS ONLY SERVES TO
FAN THEIR EMBERS. WE MOVE FROM AN ABILITY
TO SEE THE PROBLEM CLEARLY TO BECOMING
THE PROBLEM.

what they catch from their parents. A mother says, "I can't
believe I'm yelling at my children, just like my mother did. I
promised myself I would never be like her." A father says, "I've
withdrawn from intimacy in my family relationships, because I
promised myself I would never use on my children the anger
my father used on me." But because he never addresses the
source of his anger, his withdrawal becomes a moody, passive-
aggressive form of destructive anger.

And so it goes. The judgment cycle passes from generation to
generation, spreading like an infectious disease to those we love
the most.

WE LOSE OUR OBJECTIVITY IN A CRISIS AND WE BECOME THE ISSUE

When we put on a mask due to unresolved sin, we lose our
objectivity in a crisis. Everything revolves around this subjective
and distorted picture we now have of ourselves. We react out of
that warped self-portrait.

When we have unresolved sin issues, the pressure of a crisis
only serves to fan their embers. We move from an ability to see
the problem clearly to becoming the problem. This is why, in a
crisis:

▶ We become unable to read and evaluate the behavior, motives, and attitudes of others around us in a

healthy way. We can only read them in terms of their effect on us.

- We begin to demand loyalty from those over whom we have authority, at the expense of their losing a voice.

- We manipulate circumstances to our advantage.

- We blame others with a condemnation and irritation that is distorted by subjectivity.

- We create an environment dependent on our moods.

- We cause those around us to function in fear and distrust.

- We force everyone around us to grapple with two issues: how to resolve the original issue and, now, how to handle us!

When this skewed behavior takes place between parents and children, devastating consequences can result. Parents who lose objectivity teach their children to react to such behavior out of fear and self-protection. The kids unconsciously think, "The person who is supposed to nurture and protect me is the one to whom I must continually react."

When Bruce's daughter Nicole was fourteen years old, she stopped him one day as they passed each other in their family room. With the boldness of a teenager who knows she's captured some insight, she said, "Dad, you've given me permission to talk with you about your life, and I just wanted to say that when you get angry, you don't get mad or blow up. That's good. But, when you get tired or frustrated, you can get really impatient with people and hurt them with your words and

NO MATTER HOW DEEP WE TRY TO BURY IT,
UNRESOLVED SIN DOESN'T DIE. IT IS ALWAYS
ALIVE AND WELL, INFLAMING MORE SIN.

behaviors [meaning, you hurt me]. I'm not sure what to do about that."

Nicole gave her dad a true reading of his behavior in that memorable moment. Impatience is often rooted in control issues that spring from fear and blame. Under routine circumstances, Bruce can manage this inevitable effect. His unresolved sin almost seems "fixed." But, in a crisis, Bruce can lose objectivity and become the issue—as evidenced by his impatience.

WE HIDE OUR SINFUL BEHAVIOR AND BECOME VULNERABLE TO MORE SIN

Shame, blame, denial, and fear ganged up in the life of our friend Debbie. The result: an eating disorder. It damaged her body, her relationships, her college career, and then her marriage. Ashamed of what seemed to be a problem that could not possibly be true of her, Debbie denied the reality of her sin and hid her eating disorder for several years.

This cover-up became a dark breeding ground for even more eating disorders, lying, and sad attempts at failed relationships.

No matter how deep we try to bury it, unresolved sin doesn't die. It is always alive and well, inflaming more sin. Hiding creates a double whammy: It prevents us from maturing, and it makes us vulnerable to even more sin.

CUSTOM-MADE MASKS

C H A P T E R T W O

ENVIRONMENTS WITHOUT GRACE RETAIN AND
MULTIPLY UNRESOLVED SIN ISSUES.

ENVIRONMENTS THAT PROMOTE HIDING

Certain environments encourage hiding, and therefore sin. The degree to which we wear masks in our key relationships is the degree to which our character development will be thwarted. Whatever we are hiding makes us vulnerable to multiple expressions of sin. If we do not feel our home, church, or organization nurtures a safe place to reveal what is true about us, we will feel an incredible need to hide. We will think, if the penalty for disclosure is the same as getting caught, why would we ever disclose our failure? Environments without grace retain and multiply unresolved sin issues.

Wow! How many relationships are we in where the penalty for disclosing our failure is the same as getting caught? How many children have invented a polite mask to wear at home? We fashion our masks to look the way we think others would like us to appear. Meanwhile, we (and our children) are suffocating under the deceit and pain of carrying alone what we do not understand or know how to solve. Many people create this kind of destructive environment.

Bruce and Bill sat down with the leader of a Christian organization and asked what her views were on character development. Her words stunned and shocked them: "In my organization we only hire people of high character and if they demonstrate they don't have that character, we terminate them." They laughed—until they realized she wasn't kidding!

Predictably, this leader's method didn't work. Her attitude created an environment where people constantly hid their behaviors because the boss expected everyone to exhibit airtight integrity. This organization went through a long period of breakdown in relationships and productivity because, as in every family, organization, or ministry, the people in it had sin issues. The company made it unsafe for them to be honest about their struggles, and so they hid them until they eventually got caught and fired, or until they could no longer live with the duplicity and left. What a cruel joke.

In such an environment (especially one where sinning less is proof of godliness), almost everyone hides something. Hiding becomes an unspoken, almost unconscious way of life. The environment sucks the life out of truth and weakens it to the point where it cannot be applied. Hiddenness, fear, and rejection are such blaring sirens that they drown out everything else.

ROLES THAT PROMOTE HIDING

It's not only certain environments that promote hiding; some roles do too. If we could remember this simple principle—the more influence we have, the more we are tempted to hide our true selves for fear we will lose that influence—we might become less susceptible to the damage leaders in organizations, churches, or workplaces can cause when they wear masks. We have counseled leaders of associations, schools, businesses, governments, and churches who publicly condemned other leaders for their lack of integrity. Some even sued these individuals to "guard against the wolves tearing up a faithful church." Later, it came out that those who had so harshly condemned others were guilty of notable sin—deceit, theft, pornography, fraud, molestation—all under the cover of their powerful systems. It

THE GREATER THE PRIVILEGE OF INFLUENCE, THE GREATER THE TEMPTATION TO HIDE.

will always be true: The greater the privilege of influence, the greater the temptation to hide.

Those who have never learned how to apply the healing Jesus brings to their lives will always hide their sin. Hiding is naturally more serious for leaders, due to their impact on many people. Numerous Christian teachers can affirm and teach the significance of the cross, the death, and the resurrection of Jesus as the fully sufficient plan of redemption. But like a food critic without the sense of smell, many in these roles have no idea how to apply their theology to who they are. Unfortunately, this gap is harder for leaders to acknowledge because they have been elevated to positions that are too valuable to them to risk exposing the truth about themselves. The masks are never thicker or slicker.

Jeff called Bill at 3:43 A.M. from a phone booth to report that his wife had kicked him out of the house. Joan had discovered pornographic literature behind some books in his study. Jeff tried to lie his way out of the situation by telling her the magazines were from a long time ago, until she pointed out the current date on them. Jeff had been deeply enmeshed in this unresolved sin for sixteen years. At first it was just when he was out of town, but recently it had become "all the time."

At this point Jeff decided to tell Joan everything. At first she could find no words to describe her hurt. Then she started screaming loudly. Next, she slapped Jeff hard and demanded, "Get out of this house!" The extreme behavior scared Jeff. He was stunned with the horror that he had violated his wife so deeply that she resorted to violence. Bill asked Jeff to return home, where ten minutes later Bill talked with them both.

During the conversation Joan asked, "Who is this man? Is this the person I deeply trusted as my husband and father of my children? I trusted him because he appeared to live what he taught. I feel like I've been a fool."

For sixteen years, Jeff had told himself that he and God would deal with his problem privately, that someday it would stop. Many of us hold this same presumption: God and I can work alone on my stuff. I can keep this private. There is no need for disclosure to anyone else. Hiding is a really dangerous plan. Masks never work. That's like calling up the gangsters (remember those "bad guys" from the beginning of this chapter?) and inviting them over for a party. Unresolved sin leads to hiding, which makes us vulnerable to even more sinning.

Ultimately, the behavior that kept Jeff's sin unresolved—and the behavior that devastated Joan the most—wasn't Jeff's vulnerability to sinful pleasure. It was that he had tried to hide his sin from her.

When we live or work in environments that encourage hiding, we don't feel safe. If no one ever asks who we are, how we feel, why we do what we do, it is easy to hide what is true about us. As a result, we communicate primarily through our roles, not through our persons.

We will do what is expected, but that is all we will do. This is why in many organizations people can work alongside each other for years and never really know or even care who they are working with. Power, authority, position, and leverage become the unspoken means of dialogue. No one finds a place to take his or her infection out of darkness into the light where it can be deprived of its power. What a waste! What a charade! What a loss!

A MAJOR CAUSE OF BURNOUT IN AMERICANS
IS NOT OVERWORK, OVER-SCHEDULING, OR
OVER ACTIVITY. IT IS BITTERNESS.

THE EXHAUSTING WORK OF HIDING

Hiding drains us. When we hide, we can never rest. We live every waking moment with a nagging fear that someone or something will blow our cover. Hiding requires constant vigilance and maintenance. We can't stay out in public too long because our masks are in constant need of repair. After a while, we can't even remember what the masks looked like the last time we put them on.

Gradually this tension creates dysfunction in totally unrelated areas. For example, if the drain of our hiding causes us to be irritable with our family, then our guilt increases, creating added stress and energy drain. The unresolved guilt, in turn, makes us feel ashamed. This takes its toll on our mental, spiritual, and even physical health. When this happens, often one of two things results. Either we will try to get caught so we cangive up the charade, or another part of our life—one completely unrelated to our secret sin—will break down and collapse.

A major cause of burnout in Americans is not overwork, over-scheduling, or over activity. It is bitterness. The load from all the unhealed wounds we carry eventually takes its toll. The breakdowns are real and rest alone cannot heal them. Such collapses will devastate the lives of those we influence and retard their growth in trusting and loving God!

WHAT ABOUT YOU?

We're at one of those stopping points again. Time to ask you several questions and offer you some hope. Maybe you are one of the thousands who could say, "They are writing about me!" Please know that we wrote this little book to give you hope that you can begin a new way of living. If you do not have a leadership role in an organization or ministry, you still profoundly influence other people. And, you have an advantage: You will not have as great a temptation to hide.

Put a bookmark between these pages and set the book down. Before you do, ask yourself these questions:

▶ Would others who know me say I am one who tends to blame? Am I always criticizing the behaviors of others? Am I hypersensitive to people and their sins? Do I feel obliged to be their judge?

▶ Do I tend to lose my objectivity in a crisis? Do I become the issue in discussions or projects that place me under pressure or make me feel threatened?

▶ In my family, relationships, church, or work, is the penalty for disclosing what is true about me the same as getting caught? If so, how is that thwarting my character development?

Don't brush by these questions. If you are willing to face them, you could prepare yourself for a whole new way of living. And you could ignite a radical change in the way you protect and influence the lives of countless others. This stuff is that important.

The rest of the book continues to describe the painful effects of unresolved sin. If you are finding yourself in these pages, don't lose heart. God is having his way in you, even if it seems frightening and undoing. Imagine a life free from duplicity and hiding. Imagine not having to cover up what is true about you. Imagine receiving the gifts of grace that God has given you in order to heal the unresolved issues of your life. Imagine living a life without shame. Imagine feeling really alive again. That's where we're headed.

DID YOU DISCOVER?

▶ When we are unable or unwilling to resolve the sin within us, we become sensitized toward our own sin, and others' sins. We become self-appointed judges of what is wrong with other people!

▶ Our newfound sensitivity to sin actually decreases our ability to resolve the sin in our lives.

▶ Without the power of grace to deal with sin, we will ruin the spirit and violate the soul of those we claim to love and are responsible to love.

▶ Unresolved sin is always buried alive.

▶ Hiding creates a double penalty: It prevents us from maturing, and it makes us vulnerable to even more sin.

▶ The degree to which we wear a mask in our key relationships is the degree to which our character development will be thwarted.

▶ If the penalty for disclosure is the same as getting caught, we will not disclose our failures.

▶ In an environment where sinning less is proof of godliness, almost everyone hides something.

▶ Hiding drains us.

CHAPTER THREE

WHEN THE MASK SLIPS

You can't hide behind a religious mask forever; sooner or later the mask will slip and your true face will be known.

—Jesus, *The Message*
Luke 12

THE THREE-PHASE CHAIN REACTION CAUSED BY
UNRESOLVED SIN TAKES AWAY OUR ABILITY TO
HAVE INTIMATE RELATIONSHIPS. IT MAKES US
FEEL ASHAMED AND LONELY AND ROBS US OF
THE JOY OF SHOWING OUR TRUE FACE TO THE
WORLD.

Some of you may remember the science kits that parents purchased for their children at Christmas in the '60s and '70s. Today's science kits are tame by comparison. They contain things like salt, baking soda, a feather, and maybe some skin from a potato. But science kits used to contain chemicals and mysterious substances that, if mixed correctly, could take out an entire city block . . . or at least blow up the dog dish! One Saturday you'd mix a few chemicals with names like "chromium bauxite" and "manganese sulfuric tungsten" with some algae from the birdbath, and you'd burn a hole in your desk. The next day you'd mix the same chemicals with a few drops of ginger ale and you'd end up with a nasty looking boil on your hand.

Similar to a failed science experiment, it isn't pretty to watch the effects of unresolved sin in a person's life. The three-phase chain reaction caused by unresolved sin takes away our ability to have intimate relationships. It makes us feel ashamed and lonely and robs us of the joy of showing our true face to the world.

Recall the three phases of unresolved sin from chapter one:

Act of Sin

Involuntary Response

Inevitable Effect

When we sin, or someone sins against us, the act of sin evokes an involuntary response, either guilt or hurt, which causes an automatic and inevitable effect like the three we briefly considered in chapter two:

- We become highly sensitized to our sin and judge the sin of others.
- We lose our objectivity in a crisis and we become the issue.
- We hide our sinful behavior and become vulnerable to more sin.

There are other toxic byproducts that can come from choosing to hide or ignore unresolved sin. Shame, blame, fear, denial, and anger are still mixing it up. They can also produce three other debilitating results:

- We are unable to be loved or to love.
- We become vulnerable to wrong life choices.
- We attempt to control others.

WE ARE UNABLE TO BE LOVED OR TO LOVE

Wayne came to us after having been involved in a network of Christian communities whose authoritarian, legalistic leadership style caused people to feel fear, insecurity, anxiety, and weakness on the inside. On the outside, these same individuals were forceful "evangelists" who rode into town with a swagger and confronted people with gusto. Wayne was bright and affable, with plenty of talent. He had high standards and expected others to measure up to them as well.

When we met with Wayne, he gradually began to reveal his pain and hurt. As he spoke, his hands literally shook from the fearful conclusion that he was not measuring up to God's (and his leaders') spiritual standards. Never mind that he studied and prayed and memorized and fasted and served and confessed and journaled and sacrificed more than anyone we knew. Wayne was a mess—a spiritually chiseled and polished mess.

Wayne was a Christian, but he had not learned how to receive God's love. And because Wayne didn't know love, he couldn't give it to others. All of Wayne's striving left him with multiple unresolved sin issues from his past, and consequently he was obsessed with his current life, especially his ongoing cycles of progress and reversal.

Unresolved sin always causes preoccupation with our own lives. We want so badly to be mature and selfless, but our unresolved sin just keeps triggering self-centeredness. We're consumed by the need to hide the stuff we can't get right. We are driven to blame others in order to maintain our image of worth (or victim). We become self-directed, self-attentive, and self-protective. As a result, we are unable to offer love to others.

When we are preoccupied with ourselves, we don't see that our masquerade incites fear in those around us—that we become porcupines. Others consciously or unconsciously fear being intimate with us or entrusting themselves to us.

We send this involuntary, unspoken message to everyone we encounter: "I hope you like what you see. I am trying hard. But you don't really want to know me. I carry around this dark, hidden life. If you truly knew me, you'd reject me. Please, don't come too close."

Ultimately, our spouses, our friends, even our children can sense our inability to move toward them with love. How

BECAUSE WE'RE AFRAID THAT OTHERS WON'T
LOVE US IF THEY KNOW WHAT'S REALLY INSIDE
US, WE HIDE OUR JUNK. BUT HIDING THE JUNK
ALSO HIDES WHO WE ARE, WHICH KEEPS US
MORE SEPARATED FROM LOVE THAN OUR
REVEALED JUNK EVER COULD!

pitifully tragic! Because we're afraid that others won't love us if they know what's really inside us, we hide our junk. But hiding the junk also hides who we are, which keeps us more separated from love than our revealed junk ever could! Hiding from others also prevents us from receiving their love. When we choose to don a mask, we inadvertently hide our hearts from what we most desperately need—the love of others, including, and especially, God. Unless we allow others to meet our needs, we cannot receive their love. Mask-wearers are the loneliest people on the planet.

(For a fuller expression of this, you will want to read *TrueFaced Experience Edition*. See page 62 for ordering details.)

WE BECOME VULNERABLE TO WRONG LIFE CHOICES

Our friend Allison comes from a background of striving to be seen as a generous, caring, loving woman. Ten years ago the story of who she really was began to emerge. Allison was attending a new church and desperately wanted to be accepted. She started to shower people at the church with gifts. Often these gifts included cash, to assist them in their needs. With the display of such a caring and loving spirit, she was quickly given opportunities to minister to many families.

CAUGHT IN THE TRAP OF UNRESOLVED SIN
ISSUES, WE OFTEN BEGIN TO MAKE A STRING
OF POOR LIFE CHOICES, CAUSING US EVEN
MORE HARM.

After about three years of such apparent generosity, Allison
met with the leadership of her church and disclosed to them
that she had a serious problem with lying. "I'm really not the
wealthy person I would like you to believe I am." Then she
explained that she had been stealing from her employees. All
the honor, acceptance, and favor she garnered were being
funded by theft. She said, "I wanted to tell you, because my
company found out and soon I will be arrested."

The leaders asked, "Well, how much money are we talking
about?" Quietly she replied, "$93,000." Allison's unresolved
hurt from previous rejections fueled a series of wrong life
choices and resulted in months in jail.

Caught in the trap of unresolved sin issues, we often begin to
make a string of poor life choices, causing us even more harm.
Like the swindler, we try to fix our confusion and rationalize
our wrong choices in a dozen different ways.

For example:

) Unresolved shame may cause us to flee our current
situation simply to avoid the embarrassment of our
circumstances. We may move to another location
just to escape the pain.

) Unresolved blame may cause us to critique others
unfairly. We may vindictively put them down out of
a critical spirit.

) Unresolved fear, leading to insecurity, may cause us
to withhold the promotion of another or to shrink

46

from a career for which we're well suited, but for which we don't feel worthy.

▶ Unresolved denial may cause us to reject the truth about our part in a torn relationship, costing us valuable friendships, opportunities, and influence.

▶ Unresolved anger may cause us to experience burnout and to lose focus and stability. We may end up leaving a spouse or a family who are the best thing that ever happened to us.

Just ask Beth. Beth would quickly say she just loved her role on staff at her church. People loved her; the ministry was going well. But she would also now say it wasn't going as well as it was for several of her classmates from the college from which she had graduated ten years earlier. Some of them were leading large churches. A couple of them had published books. At first she would quietly ask, "Why are they doing so well and not me?" Until recently, she would never have been able to admit that she was becoming jealous of her classmates. Her jealousy drove her to want to do something as obviously successful as what they were doing. Seemingly out of the blue, she announced that she would be looking for another ministry position. She told people that she was convinced God wanted her to do this, but even her two closest mentors were somewhat taken back by her announcement.

Beth pursued a job, confident that she would be accepted for this significant change in career. She felt so confident that she gave her notice to her current employer and church. Fortunately Beth didn't get the job. It really wasn't suited for her. She defended her backfired strategy at first, until one of her mentors wisely challenged her motive. Sadly, Beth lost a

WHEN THE MASK SLIPS

CHAPTER   THREE

THE JEALOUSY, BITTERNESS, SELF-DOUBT, AND
CONFUSION THAT RESULT FROM UNRESOLVED
HURT OR GUILT CAUSE MANY TO PURSUE
SOMETHING THAT ISN'T THEM, AT THE LOSS OF
WHAT IS THEM.

wonderful opportunity to serve people who loved her and loved being with her. She made a poor choice because of the jealousy in her heart.

The jealousy, bitterness, self-doubt, and confusion that result from unresolved hurt or guilt cause many to pursue something that isn't them, at the loss of what is them. One mistaken life choice begets another.

Unresolved sin issues can seduce us into a series of wrong choices shaped primarily by current trends, media, religious experience, or persuasive pop psychology. In our unresolved and unidentified sin, we're now blindly reacting to life without perspective, guidance, or wisdom. We close down to truth that could stop the raging inevitable effects, while we open up to seductive, self-vindicating reasoning.

WE ATTEMPT TO CONTROL OTHERS

People living in the middle of the inevitable effects of unresolved sin find it impossible to submit to another, to trust another, or to allow themselves to need another person's love, because they have to be in control.

When we have been hurt or have hurt another, a deep need to be validated grows within us. We must hold onto our "rightness" at all costs, and so we strive to control every area in our life. Control validates our rightness and soothes our anger.

48 © Copyright 2005 William A. Thrall and Bruce McNicol. All rights reserved. Unauthorized duplication prohibited.

If we give up any form of control to another, we have somehow proven we must not be right and our anger will emerge. That's why the Pharisees, who were extremely controlling, revealed their politely hidden rage when Jesus challenged them about their systematic attempts to control Israel's religious and social life. Their anger erupted all over Jesus and could not be satisfied until they had him killed.

Not only must we remain in control of ourselves, but we must also control others to ensure that we don't get hurt again. We also control others to ensure that we will be seen as right, which fuels our permission to be angry. If they step out of line, our anger soon restores order. We reward or withhold approval based on how well others fit into our assessment of how they should live.

Such control is full of prejudice. Controllers have an incredible need to elevate what they believe at the expense of anything else. To continue marketing their claim of exclusive rightness, they must defame the competition.

Controllers who run organizations or churches often tell their employees or constituency that other groups are suspect and fall short of "real truth." Controllers keep repeating to themselves, "I'm it. I've got a corner on the market. Others may claim to understand some of what I know, but they can't get what they really need anywhere except from me."

Controllers create a performance-driven environment through their endless demands on how people should behave and conform. You know you're around a controller by the uneasy sense that the controller's acceptance of you can be instantly broken by a wrong behavior, a wrong allegiance, or a wrong opinion. Controllers create guarded, fearful, and edgy

PERFORMANCE-DRIVEN CULTURES CAN NEVER
PROMOTE HEALING. RATHER, THEY CREATE
MORE WOUNDING.

environments. This controlling dominance in a home, a marriage, a church, or a workplace will produce the very system Jesus condemned in the first century. Performance-driven cultures can never promote healing. Rather, they create more wounding.

José and Marcia found this out the hard way. When we met them, they both had a deep desire to honor God in their relationship with each other and with their children, but felt so broken, demeaned, and unaffirmed that nothing gave them hope. Much of their previous experiences were in performance-driven environments that were overly critical and condemning. José modeled these practices at home, deeply wounding his wife and children.

José and Marcia say, "In such performance-driven environments people never discover who they really are." This family had known very few churches that were not controlling churches. One day a friend recommended they visit a different church where they could experience a message full of grace and truth with no condemnation.

Why do people stay in churches like the one Marcia and José attended? Because they have never been taught that there is any other way to become godly. Because controlling pastors tell their congregations that submitting to them is evidence of a person's godliness. Like many other controllers, they masterfully manipulate and shame their people into submission to get their own way.

At this point you are likely identifying a home, a church, a

HEAR US WHEN WE EMPHATICALLY STATE THAT
NO CONTROLING ENVIRONMENT IS SPIRITUALLY
HEALTHY. NONE! ALL CONTROLING ENVIRON-
MENTS ARE AN EVIDENCE OF UNRESOLVED SIN.

school, a ministry, or a business run by a controller or a group
of controllers. Perhaps it's your family, church, ministry, or
workplace. Or maybe you are admitting, "I am that controller!"
Hear us when we emphatically state that no control environment is spiritually healthy. None! All control environments are
an evidence of unresolved sin.

Are we speaking about God-given convictions? Not at all.
Godly men and women have profound convictions. But when
in the name of conviction we are controlling others, we can be
sure that that conviction does not come from God. It comes
from an unresolved life issue. Don't stay in an environment
where those in responsible places need to control. No matter
how godly they may seem, their influence is like spiritual
kryptonite. It will slowly drain away your joy and leave you
forgetting who you really are.

Controllers get their way because others submit to them.
Controllers play off of the despair of people who feel helpless
or unable to fix their lives. These victims tell themselves, "If
somebody else will tell me how to live, I can hold them
responsible for my life." The deal is struck and the unspoken
agreement between victim and controller begins.

If you have ever been in such an environment, you know that
no one takes off his or her mask voluntarily. The gamble of
authenticity is way too high, because if the real you ever
showed up, you'd be ridiculed and then sent away to fold socks
until you got your act together.

PARENTS WHO HAVEN'T DEALT WITH THEIR OWN
UNRESOLVED ISSUES ARE NOT ABLE TO GIVE
DIRECTION TO THEIR TEENAGERS AT THE MOST
CRITICAL TIMES IN THEIR LIVES.

Why do people feel compelled to control everything around
them? You should know this one by now—unresolved sin.
Various inevitable effects have teamed up to convince the
controller that he or she has been deeply wronged. Controllers
must be "right." It is their highest value. Their assessment of
truth becomes the standard of judgment by which everyone
they influence must live. What's really tragic is that these
controllers probably have been wronged. But their blind com-
mitment to being right keeps them from being healed of the
wrong done against them, and everyone they influence pays.

A GREAT LOSS OF OPPORTUNITY

When these inevitable effects rule our lives, others must live
without our direction or ability to give them hope. Parents who
haven't dealt with their own unresolved issues are not able to
give direction to their teenagers at the most critical times in
their lives. They simply don't have enough time, confidence, or
freedom from their own shame to give guidance. As a result,
high-school kids help each other grow up because their parents
are so preoccupied with their own life issues. It's really hard for
parents who haven't grown up to try to "grow up" their children. They can make judgments, give advice, even turn them to
God and his Word, but they cannot with any confidence or
conviction give their kids hope.

The parents of an easygoing young teen told Bruce that their son displayed patterns of unexpected, uncontrollable anger. This respected couple related how their son's anger had repeatedly embarrassed them in public. As Bruce listened to their story, he found himself connecting the dots of family influence. They recounted their own struggle to forgive those who had defrauded them in business dealings. Their initial disappointment festered into solidified resentment and bitterness. They verbally abused and ridiculed those who had wronged them. The load of hatred spilled over into their daily dealing with others.

Where did this pattern emerge? From a previous generation of parents who had packed their lives with unforgiveness, anger, and verbal abuse. Now, this son, who didn't have the experience or objectivity to live independently from his parents, unconsciously responded to his own issues of hurt with anger and resentment. This is where his "unexplained fits of frenzied anger" came from.

When we have unresolved sin, we rob others of the opportunity to heal and mature in those same areas of our unresolved sin. One of the greatest opportunities we have as humans is to give others hope that the painful and destructive issues of life can be resolved. But if we have unresolved sin, we can never transfer the reality of that hope. We also cannot give direction to others struggling with sin when we are trapped in our own. Whew! Take a moment to contemplate the reality of that last sentence on those you influence.

WHAT ABOUT YOU?

The companion volume to this little book, *TrueFaced Experience Edition*, focuses on a process of hope that explores

THE COMPANION VOLUME TO THIS LITTLE
BOOK, *TRUEFACED EXPERIENCE EDITION*, FOCUSES ON A
PROCESS OF HOPE THAT EXPLORES HOW GOD
IN HIS GRACE HAS GIVEN US A REDEMPTIVE
SOLUTION TO THE PROBLEM OF UNRESOLVED
SIN. TRUEFACED TAKES A FRESH LOOK AT THE
LOVE, REPENTANCE AND FORGIVENESS WE CAN
EXPERIENCE WHEN WE TAKE OFF OUR MASKS
AND START LIVING IN THE OPEN.

how God in his grace has given us a redemptive solution to the problem of unresolved sin. *TrueFaced Experience Edition* takes a fresh look at the love, repentance and forgiveness we can experience when we take off our masks and start living in the open.

What we want to leave you with for now is a recap of how the inevitable effects of unresolved sin may have worked themselves into the fabric of your life. Perhaps you're thinking, "This information has helped me understand why some of the people in my life are the way they are, but I really can't see myself in these pages. I'm not aware that unresolved sin has caused me to feel shame, blame, fear, denial, and anger. I don't think I have kept others from loving me or that I have a need to control."

If this is you, we have a brief exercise for you. Sit down at the computer or grab some paper and a pen.

1. Think of a time when you acted in sin or when an act of sin was committed against you. The more vivid and real, the more profound this exercise will be. This is for no one else to read. This is for you and God to review.

2. Describe what the sin was (the act of sin) and its initial impact on you (the involuntary responses)—either guilt or hurt.

3. Now, here is the most important part: If you haven't resolved the guilt or the hurt, describe why. What caused God's healing to get skipped, moving you from the involuntary responses right into the involuntary effects of shame, blame, fear, denial, or anger? Remember, unresolved sin causes a nagging sense in your heart that doesn't go away.

Some of you will recall acts of sin done against you as a child. Perhaps the offender was a person you trusted, someone you were helpless against. You were too young to be able to identify, understand, or resolve what was happening to you, but the damage happened and you experienced lasting, internal effects. Now, as an adult, you must face that effect and damage, and allow for God's healing. He has not forgotten the event. He has not forgotten you. And he has appointed a time to redeem what seems unredeemable. As perfectly as he planned the most incredible sunset, he has planned for your freedom.

We encourage you not only to understand and identify what your offender did but how his or her act of sin affected you. Has it defined who you have become?

Or perhaps you recall acts of sin done against you in adulthood. You knew you were hurt, but somehow gave yourself permission to let the hurt and guilt go unresolved. What caused you to skip God's healing at the involuntary responses stage, moving you into the involuntary effects of shame, blame, fear, denial, or anger? What left you feeling resentment, bitterness, or perhaps alienated from a relationship?

Allow yourself to relive that season. As best you can remember, jot down the emotions, feelings, and attitudes that have since emerged. For your sake and for the sake of all you influence, don't give "super-spiritualized" answers that deny the pain.

IF YOU HAVE ALLOWED GOD TO HELP YOU CAPTURE HOW UNRESOLVED SIN AND ITS PROCESS HAS AFFECTED YOU, IF YOU CAN SEE YOUR PATTERNS OF SELF-PROTECTION AND HIDDENNESS, THEN YOU ARE READY TO FOLLOW THE SIGN THAT LEADS TO THE BEAUTIFUL CITY CALLED HOPE. FOR A DETAILED ROADMAP OF THE JOURNEY, PICK UP COPIES OF TRUEFACED EXPERIENCE EDITION, TRUEFACED EXPERIENCE GUIDE AND THE TRUEFACED EXPERIENCE DVD SET, THE COMPANIONS TO THE BOOK. SEE PAGE 62 FOR ORDERING DETAILS.

4. Finally, what specific life patterns ensnared you as a result? In chapters two and three we gave an overview of six of the dozens of specific life patterns and difficulties. You may see yourself in one or more of these, or God may bring other behaviors or patterns to mind. We hope that as a result of doing this exercise, you will agree with the following statements:

- My shame, blame, fear, denial, or anger did not just appear out of thin air.
- I am able to take myself on a really profound and terrible journey.
- I lose my objectivity and perspective somewhere on this journey.
- I make really dumb choices and life decisions along this journey.
- I forfeit the love of those closest to me on this journey.
- I become incredibly judgmental of the sins of others during this journey.
- I grow tired and miserable and alone during this journey.

If you have allowed God to help you capture how unresolved

sin and its process has affected you, if you can see your patterns of self-protection and hiddenness, then you are ready to follow the sign that leads to the beautiful city called Hope.

For a detailed roadmap of the journey, pick up copies of *TrueFaced Experience Edition*, and the *TrueFaced Experience Guide*, the workbook companion to the book. See page 62 for ordering details.

DID YOU DISCOVER?

▶ The three-phase chain reaction that results from unresolved sin removes our ability to have intimate relationships with others.

▶ We deeply want to be mature and selfless, but our unresolved sin keeps triggering self-centeredness.

▶ Unresolved shame may cause us to move to another location to escape pain.

▶ Unresolved denial may cause us to reject the truth about our part in a torn relationship, costing us valuable friendships, opportunities, and influence.

▶ People living with the inevitable effects of unresolved sin must be in control. They find it impossible to submit to another, to trust another, or to allow themselves to need another's love.

▶ Controllers create performance-driven environments through their endless demands on how people should behave and conform.

▶ Performance-driven cultures can never promote healing. Rather, they create more wounding.

WHEN THE MASK SLIPS

C H A P T E R   T H R E E

▶ When in the name of "conviction" we control others, we can be sure that conviction does not come from God.

▶ Parents who haven't dealt with their own unresolved issues are not able to give direction to their children at the most critical times in their lives.

▶ One of the greatest opportunities we have is to give others hope that the painful and destructive issues of life can be resolved.

▶ Our shame, blame, fear, denial, or anger comes from specific unresolved life issues.

WHEN THE MASK SLIPS

C H A P T E R   T H R E E

▶ When in the name of "conviction" we control others, we can be sure that conviction does not come from God.

▶ Parents who haven't dealt with their own unresolved issues are not able to give direction to their children at the most critical times in their lives.

▶ One of the greatest opportunities we have is to give others hope that the painful and destructive issues of life can be resolved.

▶ Our shame, blame, fear, denial, or anger comes from specific unresolved life issues.

▶ When in the name of "conviction" we control others, we can be sure that conviction does not come from God.

▶ Parents who haven't dealt with their own unresolved issues are not able to give direction to their children at the most critical times in their lives.

▶ One of the greatest opportunities we have is to give others hope that the painful and destructive issues of life can be resolved.

▶ Our shame, blame, fear, denial, or anger comes from specific unresolved life issues.

ABOUT THE AUTHORS

BILL THRALL
serves as leadership mentor for Leadership Catalyst, (LCI) and as a director on LCI's board. Prior to LCI, Bill led Open Door Fellowship in Phoenix, a church he established in 1973. Bill is also the coauthor of *The Ascent of a Leader, Beyond Your Best* (Jossey Bass), and *TrueFaced Experience Edition* (Navpress) and continues to speak to people around the world about issues of trust, mentoring, and leadership. Bill lives in Phoenix with his wife, Grace. They have three children and nine grandchildren.

BRUCE McNICOL
guides Leadership Catalyst as president, combining international work experience and degrees in finance law, theology and organizational development. He is a respected teacher and mentor for both established and emerging leaders in multiple cultures and contexts. Also the coauthor of *The Ascent of a Leader, Beyond Your Best* (Jossey Bass) and *TrueFaced Experience Edition* (Navpress). Bruce is active as a speaker and mentor around the world. He lives in Phoenix with his wife, Janet. They have three children.

JOHN LYNCH
serves on Leadership Catalyst's staff, speaking, filming, and writing with Bill and Bruce. He is also a contributing editor to *Beyond Your Best* (Jossey Bass) and *TrueFaced Experience Edition* (Navpress). John is the teaching pastor at Open Door Fellowship, and co-founder of Sharkey Productions, a drama outreach in Phoenix. He is a playwright and storyteller, and lives in Phoenix with his wife, Stacey. They have three children.

One word has the power to catalyze greatness in an individual, an organization, or a nation: *Trust.*

Surveys show that trust is the #1 requirement for influence in life and leadership. But for many, trust has been hard to come by or misplaced.

The *mission* of Leadership Catalyst is to *build and restore trust in leaders and in those they influence.* Established in 1995, Leadership Catalyst is recognized as an international resource for helping leaders learn how to develop relationships of trust and environments of grace.

Email: info@leadershipcatalyst.org

LEADERSHIP
CATALYST

Website: www.leadershipcatalyst.org

Voice: 888-249-0700 Toll-free in North America
Voice: 602-249-7000
Fax: 602-249-0611

Address: 1600 E. Northern Avenue, Suite 280
Phoenix, AZ 85020

ABOUT *HIGH TRUST CULTURE*™ RESOURCES

Leadership Catalyst offers *High Trust Culture*™ resources for all audiences.

For the Individual: Leadership Catalyst offers a variety of resource tools to help you build trust in your friendships, your family, and your community. Visit our web site at www.leadershipcatalyst.org for more information about our self-guiding resources.

For the Organization: The *High Trust Culture*™ process is for major organizations, schools, churches and institutions in which the CEO or senior leader makes a choice for cultural change which will re-shape the way people, teams and leaders are developed.

The *High Trust Culture*™ process functions much like a computer operating system that accelerates all other programs in the computer. Delivery of the *High Trust Culture*™ process is either self-guided or facilitated by Leadership Catalyst's team during an intensive multi-month residential and tele-coaching program, beginning with the CEO and key members of their executive team, then moving into their organization. Visit www.leadershipcatalyst.org for details of the *High Trust Culture*™ process.

Leadership Catalyst's High Trust principles can impact all areas of life. Here are a few of the results that you can experience:

- Better prepare children to make wise, life choices.
- Develop stronger character, self-worth and esteem.
- Respect and protect each person's limitations.
- Improve honesty and trust.
- Help each other identify and pursue life purpose.
- Develop high-quality, long-lasting relationships.
- Go beyond short-term conflict resolution to long-term reconciliation.
- Enhance appreciation for each person's unique contributions.
- Create dynamic teams in place of personal agendas.
- Increase team effectiveness and productivity.
- Expand influence with customers, partners and other organizations.

TrueFaced Experience Guide
Workbook companion to the TrueFaced: Experience Edition. The TrueFaced Experience Guide is designed to be use with the TrueFaced Experience DVD, which provides additional content, stories and directions to lead your small group in the TrueFaced Experience.

TrueFaced Experience DVD & Leaders Handbook
The TrueFaced Experience DVD and Leaders Handbook provide additional content, powerful TrueFaced stories and instructions to lead your small group in the Truefaced Experience.

TrueFaced Experience Small Group Pack
The TrueFaced Small Group Pack includes:
8 TrueFaced Experience Edition Books
8 TrueFaced Experience Guides
1 TrueFaced Experience DVD
1 TrueFaced Leaders Handbook
1 set of TrueFaced QuEW Cards

TrueFaced Experience Edition
By Bill Thrall, Bruce McNicol, John Lynch
Completely revised edition of the best-selling book, TrueFaced, designed to facilitate group interaction and implementation of the principles when used with the TrueFaced Experience DVD and the TrueFaced Experience Guide.

TrueFaced Experience Leader Pack
The TrueFaced Experience is changing small groups, families, marriages, churches and organizations around the world.
The Leader Pack includes:
1 TrueFaced Experience Edition Book
1 TrueFaced Experience Guide
1 TrueFaced Experience DVD
1 TrueFaced Leaders Handbook
1 set of TrueFaced QuEW Cards

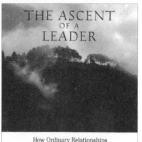

The Ascent of a Leader
How Ordinary Relationships Develop Extraordinary Character and Influence
By Bill Thrall, Bruce McNicol, Ken McElrath
Hardcover, 224 pages

Beyond Your Best
Develop Your Relationships, Fulfill Your Destiny
By Bill Thrall, Ken McElrath, Bruce McNicol
Paperback, 160 pages

The Ascent of a Leader Experience Guide
This biblically based 8-module experience provides a powerful small group process that explores the principles from the book *The Ascent of a Leader*. The Ascent of a Leader Experience is an engaging, interactive experience that is ideal for any size group including marriages, small groups, mentoring relationships, ministry teams and Sunday School classes.

The TrueFaced Message CD
An introduction to *TrueFaced* featuring the powerful message by John Lynch. (45 minutes)

The TrueFaced Message Cassette
An introduction to *TrueFaced* featuring the powerful message by John Lynch. (45 minutes)

Experiencing Affirmation in Your Marriage
Includes two booklets containing teaching and tools for
a husband and wife to experience the power of affirming
one another.

**Experiencing
Affirmation in
Your Family**
Includes four booklets
containing teaching
and tools for a family
to experience the
power of affirming
one another.
Appropriate for all
ages. (Please order one
booklet per family
member.)

Affirming Each Other-High Trust Teams™
Use this tool to experience the power of affirming
one another in your small group or team. (Please
order one tool for each team member.)

To order or for other resources and special offers,
call the Leadership Catalyst
Toll-Free Order Line:
1.888.249.0700 or online:
www.leadershipcatalyst.org